Introduction

This book contains a variety of recipes for meat dishes representing national cuisine of various countries. Some of them are easy to make and some are not but it is always nice to cook something new, isn't it?

Thanks to this book you will be able to cook your own "home-style" and surprisingly delicious dishes. Recipes in this book are excellent for festive parties and for typical home lunches and dinners.

The book provides 40 recipes for meat dishes and 14 culinary tricks that will take cooking to a restaurant level.

I hope my recipes will help you diversify your "cooking" life starting from today! Treat yourself, your friends and beloved ones!

Pork with Onion

Pork with Onion is a dish quite easy and, most importantly, quick to cook.
The more kinds of onions, the better as they make the dish rich and hearty. To be served with noodles, rice or beans.

To make Pork with Onion you will need

Pork. 300 g. It's better to take the neck or the ribs.
Onion. Yellow, red and white 1 pieces each.
Green onions. A few large bunches.
Garlic. 2 cloves.
Soy sauce. 2-3 tablespoons (50-70 ml).
Rice vinegar. 1 tablespoon.
Sesame oil. ½ teaspoon.
Sugar. 2 teaspoons.
Ground black pepper. To taste.
Ground ginger. To taste.

Cooking Pork with Onion

Finely slice the garlic and 2 bunches of green onions.
Mix sugar, vinegar, garlic, black pepper, ground ginger, green onions and sesame oil in a bowl.
Add soy sauce and stir it all thoroughly.
Cut the pork into thin wide slices.
Put the meat in the marinade and leave it for 20-30 minutes.
Chop the onion.
Preheat a couple of tablespoons of vegetable oil in a large frying pan.
Take the meat from the marinade and put it in the pan. Do not pour out the marinade.
Fry the pork until it changes color and fried sites appear.
Then add chopped onion.
Stir, wait until the onion is fried and add the marinade.
Stew the meat until the marinade evaporates, stirring it from time to time.

Pork in Bazhe Sauce

Bazhe, a walnut-garlic sauce, is often used in Georgian cuisine and is suitable for meat, fish and vegetables. **Pork in bazhe sauce** is an aromatic and slightly spicy but very tasty dish, served both hot and cold.

To make Pork in Bazhe Sauce you will need

Pork. 1 kg. I recommend the blade.
Onion. 3 pcs.
Walnuts. 100 g.
Pomegranate juice. 50 ml and some pomegranate seeds.
Garlic. 2 cloves.
Fresh cilantro. To taste.
Grape vinegar 6%. 1 tablespoon.
Milled grain coriander. ½ teaspoon.
Imereti saffron. 1 teaspoon.
Salt. To taste.
Ground black pepper. To taste.
Water. 500 ml.

Cooking Pork in Bazhe Sauce

Trim the fat off the pork if any.
Cut the meat into small pieces.

Cut 2 onions in half-rings.

Heat a little of vegetable oil in a deep frying pan and fry the pork until it changes color, add chopped onion and sprinkle with salt and pepper.

Cook at medium heat until the onions are soft.

Add 500 ml of water and simmer the pork covered at low heat until cooked, for about 1 hour.

While the pork is stewing, process with **bazhe sauce**.

Cut the remaining onion into small dices and fry it.

Grind the walnuts in a blender.

Randomly chop the garlic and spread into the blender, add a little salt and grind.

Squeeze the onions that are fried through a sieve into a bowl where the bazhe sauce will be made. You don't need the onions in the sauce, only their juice. The onion juice can be put into the pan where pork is being stewed.

Add grind nuts, garlic, spices, salt and ground black pepper, pomegranate juice, vinegar, coriander and saffron.

Mix well and bring the sauce to the consistency of a liquid sour cream, slowly pouring boiling water.

When the meat is completely stewed, remove the lid from the pan. Cook without cover to reduce fluid if there is any left in the pan.

Pour the bazhe sauce over the pork, stir.

Let the sauce warm up in the pan for 5-7 minutes and turn off the flame.

Leave it for another 10 minutes.

Sprinkle the finished dish with chopped cilantro and pomegranate seeds and serve.

Yahni

Yahni or **yahne** is a Georgian or rather Adjarian dish. It's in the form of a thickened soup, something between a soup and sauteed meat and vegetables, very spicy and hearty. To make a perfect, traditional **yahni** we will use beef and it's important to take mature meat, so veal won't be suitable. Also, if you don't have tomato paste, you can easily replace it with thick tomato juice. Anyhow, the dish will be delicious.

To make Yahni you will need

Beef. 1½ kg. Beef brisket will be great.
Onion. 300-400 g.
Nuts. Walnuts. 120-150 g.
Garlic. 4-5 cloves.
Tomato paste. 1 tablespoon.
Tomato juice. 200 ml.
Butter. 50 g.
Flakes of hot red pepper. 1 teaspoon or to taste.
Imereti saffron (marigold) - 1½ teaspoon.
Ground coriander. ¾-1 teaspoon.
Ground black pepper. ½ teaspoon or to taste.
Salt. To taste.

Cooking Yahni

Cut the beef into medium-sized pieces.

Put the meat in a pot, pour boiling water just to cover the meat and cook for 40-60 minutes. At the end of the cooking salt the broth to taste.

Fry walnuts in a dry pan for about a minute, until you can smell a beautiful walnut scent.

Put the nuts and almost all the spices, except for the half of Imereti saffron, to the blender and grind into a homogeneous mass.

Grind the second half of Imereti saffron separately.

Cut onions into thin slices along fibers. This method will let the onions dissolve in the sauce. If you cut them across the fibers into half rings, some parts of the onion will remain as a whole.

Take the boiled meat out from the pot and put it in a large frying pan with hot butter. Leave the broth in the pot.

Fry the meat until light golden brown.

Spread all the onions on the meat and gently season with salt.

Simmer meat in onions under cover at a very low heat. Don't add any liquid but if the onions and meat begin to fry then add a couple of tablespoons of broth. The meat will stew for another 50 minutes.

Heat the remaining butter in a small pan and add grind Imereti saffron.

Stir and heat at medium heat for 30 seconds, add tomato juice. Fry the mass, stirring quickly to prevent burning. Add it to the meat.

Stir and continue to stew.

If the fluid evaporates, add a little broth.

Add 2-3 ladles of broth to the nut mass.

Stir and add more broth if necessary, so that the sauce has a consistency of liquid sour cream.

Pour the sauce to the stewing meat and mix it all well.

Finely dice garlic.

About 15 minutes after the nut sauce is added to the meat, spread chopped garlic, stir and cover again.

Stew for another 5 minutes and remove from heat.

Pork Marinated in Tangerines

Pork Marinated in Tangerines - this dish goes well with almost any garnish, but it tastes best with fried vegetables. Crispy breading makes the meat tender and spicy.

To make Pork Marinated in Tangerines you will need

Pork. 300 g. The best will be neck.
Tangerine. 1 pc.
Soy sauce. 30 ml.
Garlic. 1 clove.
Breadcrumbs.
Salt. To taste.
Ground black pepper. To taste.

Cooking Pork in Tangerines

Squeeze the tangerine. Don't throw the peels.
Dice the garlic finely.
Mix the squeezed juice, garlic and soy sauce in a small bowl. Season the marinade with pepper.
Chop the meat into strips. Dip the meat in the marinade, adding tangerine peels.
The marinade should be just enough for the meat to absorb it completely.
Let the meat marinate for 2 to 8 hours – the longer, the better.
Take the meat from the marinade; coat the meat evenly in breadcrumbs.
Fry the meat in vegetable oil in a saucepan until breadcrumbs are caramel brown and crispy.
Pork marinated in tangerines is ready.

Oven-Braised Beef Ribs

Preparation of **Oven-Braised Beef Ribs** does take a lot of time but in the end we enjoy a very soft and full-flavored meat with a wonderful sauce. Unlike beef stew, which is cooked on the stove not in the oven, meat in this dish has a more intense taste; it's softer and keeps its one-piece shape. This method of braising beef ribs is popular in France where I learned this recipe.

To cook Oven-Braised Beef Ribs you will need

Beef ribs. 1 kg.
Onion. 200-300 g.
Carrot. 1 pc.
Garlic. 1-2 cloves.
Black peppercorns. 1 teaspoon.
Vegetable oil. 50 ml.
Salt. To taste.

Cooking Oven-Braised Beef Ribs

Cut the beef ribs into pieces in the middle between the ribs.
Slice onions along the fibers.
Heat vegetable oil in a deep frying pan. This cookware will be then put in the oven, so choose the appropriate one.
Fry the pieces of beef ribs on all sides in vegetable oil until golden brown.
When the edges have browned, add the chopped onions and the carrot sliced diagonally.
Add salt and put about 1 teaspoon of black peppercorns.
Cut cloves of garlic in half, and just add them to the meat.
Stir and fry the onion until transparent.
Add a little hot water so that the pieces of meat are about half covered.

With a spatula, scraping all fried pieces of meat.
Close the dish with a very tight cover or foil the dish with aluminum foil.
Put the pan in the oven, preheated to 160 °C - 170 °C and cook for about 2-2½ hours.
The most important thing is to prevent the moisture from evaporating from under the cover or the foil, so check it in a half-hour and add hot water if necessary.
In 2-2½ hours the beef is fully braised.
The ribs should separate from the meat easily, almost without effort.

Pork in Sweet and Sour Sauce

This pork is easy to make at home and the dish doesn't require any fancy ingredients. Although there are a lot of ingredients, they are simple and easy to buy.

To make Pork in Sweet and Sour Sauce you will need

Pork. 300 g.
Pineapples, fresh or canned. 150 g.
1 egg.
Sugar. 1 tablespoon.
Corn starch. 4 tablespoon.
1 orange.
Lemon. ½ pc.

Ketchup. 1 tablespoon.
Bulgarian pepper. 2 pcs. Preferably of various colors.
Onion. 1 pc.
Carrot. 1 pc.
Garlic. 2 cloves.
Soy sauce. 50 ml.
Rice vinegar. 50 ml.
Green onions. A few leaves.
Ground black pepper. To taste.
Salt. To taste.

Cooking Pork in Sweet and Sour Sauce

Chop the pork into small pieces, about 1 cm thick.
Pour 2 tablespoons of starch in a deep dish and add an egg into it. Sprinkle a little salt and pepper.
Mix the egg with the starch to obtain batter.
Put the pork to the batter, mix it well and leave it for the time of preparation of the remaining ingredients.
Since the dish needs to prepared quickly - chop all the remaining ingredients at once, otherwise there will be no time afterwards.
Dice the garlic very finely.
Cut the onions into large chunks.
Chop the Bulgarian pepper coarsely as well.
Cut the pineapple into small pieces.
Clean the carrot and cut it into thin slices.

Squeeze the juice of a whole orange and half lemon. Seeds, if any, should be removed.
Preheat vegetable oil in a frying pan.
Pour a spoon or spoon and a half of the starch in a bowl and dip the pieces of pork in batter in it.
Put a few pieces of pork in a frying pan and begin to fry it. It's possible and even necessary to fry the meat in parts, so that it is fried and not stewed in its own juice.

Fry on both sides until cooked and strong golden brown.

Spread the fried pork on a plate covered with a paper towel to soak up the excess of oil.

Heat another pan and put the garlic in it.

Fry it quickly, and then add onion and carrot. Stirring constantly, fry them for fifteen minutes, and then add Bulgarian pepper. Fry all together, often stirring, then add tomato sauce, soy sauce, sugar and vinegar to the vegetables.

Stir again until tomato sauce and sugar dissolve, then add pineapple and orange and lemon juice.

Let it simmer for a couple of minutes and add the meat. Stir all well again, and then quickly dissolve the remaining starch - about half a tablespoon - with cold water and pour into the pan.

Stir again, making the starch sauce thick, and turn off the heat.

Spread the meat on plates and serve it, sprinkling with green onions.

Rice will be the best for garnish.

Pork Knuckle in Beer

It takes quite a long time to cook **pork knuckle in beer** – about 4-4½ hours but it doesn't require much effort, so the dish is worth to spend time on it.

The combination of crispy fried pork skin and soft, tender meat, spices aroma and smell of dark beer are unlikely to leave anyone indifferent.

To make Pork Knuckle in Beer you will need

Pork knuckle. 1-2 pcs.
Dark beer. 500 ml.
Carrot. 1 pc.
Celery root.
Onion. 1 medium bulb.
Garlic. Several cloves.
1 tomato.
Parsley. A small bunch.

Salt. To taste.
Sugar or honey. 2 tablespoons.
Caraway. To taste.
Rosemary. To taste.
Bay leaf. 2-3 pcs.
Black peppercorns. 1 teaspoon.

Cooking Pork Knuckle in Beer

Chop all the vegetables except for garlic. The garlic should be just cleaned and cut in half. Bind the bunch of parsley with a string.

Sprinkle a little salt on a cutting board and press the chopped garlic against salt with effort. Salt adheres well to the cut side.

Using a thin knife make small incisions in the knuckle along the bone, without touching the skin. Insert garlic with salt in resulting holes. This way, the meat will get salt from the inside during cooking.

Put the knuckle into the saucepan; add all the chopped vegetables, thyme, rosemary, salt, black peppercorns and bay leaf.

Pour 250 ml of dark beer into the saucepan, and then add some water so the liquid covers the meat almost completely.

Heat up the pan, bring to a boil and cook at medium heat, at a very low boil for about two and a half hours. If the liquid boils out, pour a little boiling water.

Take the cooked knuckle out of the broth and let it cool down.

Add 2 tablespoons of sugar or honey to the remaining 250 ml of beer and stir until completely dissolved.

Preheat the oven to 220ºC - 230ºC.

Put the meat on a baking pan and glaze it with half of the beer and honey or sugar mixture.

Place the baking pan in the oven. Glaze again with the remaining mixture in 15-20 minutes and turn the heat down to 190ºC-200ºC.

Cook the knuckle for about an hour / an hour and a half, the longer in the oven, the softer the meat will get but do not overcook.

Use potatoes or sauerkraut as garnish. Serving the dish with mustard is a must!

Minced Meat Schnellklops

There are many dishes made of minced meat as it's a pretty easy-to-use and easy-to-cook product. However, it's always possible to cook an unusual dish even from the most usual ingredient, if you take it as a basis. I encourage you to try out "schnellklops", a German dish. It's simple and quick to prepare.

To make Minced Meat Schnellklops you will need

For 2 servings.

Minced meat or mince from poultry. 250 g.
Onion. 2 medium bulbs.
Flour. 1 tablespoon.
Sour cream. 150 ml. The fatter, the better.
Salt. To taste.
Black pepper freshly ground. To taste.

Cooking Minced Meat Schnellklops

Dice the onion.
Heat a little vegetable oil in a deep frying pan and fry the onion. Add black pepper and salt.

Once the onion starts to become transparent, add minced meat. Mix it with the onions and fry all together, mashing large pieces of minced into really small ones with a spatula.

When the liquid from the beef evaporates and the pieces of minced meat begin to fry, sprinkle a tablespoon of flour overt the meat.

Mix the flour with meat and let it fry a little, just a minute or two, constantly stirring. Flour will thicken the sauce and if you gently roast it, you will get rid of the taste of raw flour.

It's best to mix sour cream with a few tablespoons of milk before adding to the pan. Thus, the cream will not curl when added to the hot stew.

Turn the heat down to very low and add sour cream to the roasted meat.

Mix and stew the dish at very low heat for 10-15 minutes. The sauce should just barely boil. Otherwise, the sour cream, despite the pre-mix with milk, can still curl and sauce will fail to be smooth and creamy.

Schnellklops is usually served with boiled potatoes.

The dish turns out very soft, tasty and rich in flavor. Children will love it, too!

Home-Made Ham

Except for a long cooking time, **home-made ham** has no other cons at all. Preparing the pork ham for cooking in the oven does not take much time or effort, the only thing you have to do is to put the piece of pork in the oven. How simple is that?

It's completely up to you how you wish to serve home-made ham. It may be the main hot dish, cold slices on a festive buffet, one of the ingredients of the sandwiches and canapes or of a great royal breakfast.

To make Home-Made Ham you will need

Pork. Leg in one piece. 1½ kg.
Sour cream. 2 tablespoons.
Mustard. 1 tablespoon.
Paprika. 3 teaspoons with a heap.
Ground black pepper. To taste.

Hot peppers. To taste.
Salt. To taste.

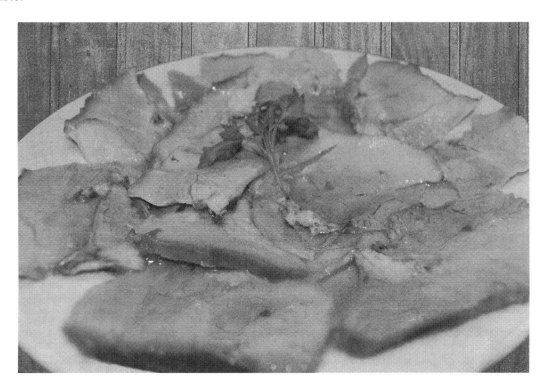

Cooking Home-Made Ham

Clean the garlic and cut in half, lengthwise.
Make small incisions in a piece of pork leg with a thin knife, add a little salt and push a half of a garlic clove in each incision.
Rub salt over the meat.
In a small pan, spread sour cream, paprika, black and hot pepper, a little salt and mustard.
Cream it all together until smooth.
Place the meat on a foil and pour the marinade over it.
Wrap the pork in foil, place it in a casserole or an oven-pan and cook in the oven, pre-heat to 200°C.
Cook the pork counting 30 minutes per 500 g + another 25 minutes. For our 1½ kilo we will need 2 hours.
After about half of the basic cooking time, reduce the oven temperature to 180°C.
For the remaining 25 minutes of cooking, open or cut the foil and let the meat roast on top.
When the time is up, take the **meat** out of the oven, and cover it with a sheet of foil and leave to cool.
After 10-15 minutes you can slice it if you want to serve it hot.
Ham is usually served with mustard and horseradish.

Ćevapi (Ćevapčići)

Ćevapčići or **ćevapi** is a dish of the peoples of the Balkan Peninsula. It's fried sausages made of minced meat with onions and spices.
Ćevapčići is served with plenty of sliced onion rings and fresh white bread. Sliced tomatoes and fried potatoes are also served as garnish.

To make Ćevapčići you will need

Minced meat. Beef, a mix of beef and pork or mutton mince is usually used. 500 g.
Onion. One very large bulb.
Garlic. 1 clove.
Soda. ½ teaspoon.

Black pepper freshly ground. To taste.
Salt. To taste.

Cooking Ćevapčići

Clean the onions and dice very finely.
Ground the garlic in a blender.
Mix all the ingredients: beef, chopped onion, garlic, baking soda, salt and freshly ground black pepper in a bowl. Use your hands to mix it long and carefully, at least 10 minutes, until it becomes very sticky.
Film the bowl and put it to the fridge for at least 2-3 hours, preferably overnight.
Form small sausages, 7-8 centimeters long and 2 centimeters thick.
Preheat a grill pan.
Grease the pan with vegetable oil and fry the sausages on all sides until cooked.
While the sausages are frying, slice the onions into thin rings.
Place the sausages on a plate, richly garnish with onions, sprinkle with finely chopped parsley and serve.

Pork Chops in Mustard

Pork absorbs flavors of marinades and spices quite well so it's possible to get a different taste of meat only by changing some of the ingredients or the entire composition of the marinade. Mustard marinade, with all its simplicity, not only adds to the taste of pork, but also makes the meat tenderer.

To make Pork Chops in Mustard you will need

Pork neck. 800 g.
Mustard. 2 tablespoons with a small heap.
Flour. 2-3 tablespoons.
Garlic. 1-2 cloves.
Salt. To taste.
Black pepper freshly ground. To taste.

Cooking Pork Chops in Mustard

Chop the meat into pieces 2-2½ cm thick.
Tenderize the meat.
Dice the garlic finely enough.
Spread the tenderized meat in a deep bowl and add a couple of tablespoons of mustard. It's best to use normal spicy mustard. Also add chopped garlic and black pepper freshly ground.
Mix it all thoroughly so that the mustard, pepper and garlic evenly cover all the meat chops.
Let the meat marinate for at least 1 hour.

Preheat vegetable oil in a large frying pan.

Season the meat with salt on both sides to taste and roll in flour.

Spread the chops in the hot frying pan so they don't touch each other.

Fry the pork until cooked at medium heat.

Mustard spiciness will disappear almost completely during frying and the **pork chops** will be tender and aromatic.

Hebrew-Style Meat

I do not know if this recipe fairly belongs to the Jewish cuisine but it was presented to me like one. **Hebrew-Style Meat** is a savory and hearty dish for everyday meal at home. It's easy to cook, although cooking takes a lot of time, 2-2 ½ hours, depending on the quality of meat.

To make Hebrew-Style Meat you will need

Beef. 1 kg.
Onion. 1 kg.
Black peppercorns. 1 teaspoon.
Bay leaf. 2 pcs.
Salt. To taste.
Vegetable oil for frying.

Cooking Hebrew-Style Meat

Dice the onion finely.

Heat vegetable oil in a deep saucepan and spread the chopped onion.

Cut the beef into small pieces as well.

Stir and fry the onion until light golden.

Add the meat to the onions.

Stir at medium heat and continue to fry.

At first, meat will give away a lot of juice. Fry all together, stirring, until the juice has evaporated and the meat starts to fry.

Add cold water to enhance the taste of the future sauce, bring to a boil, cover and continue to simmer at a very low heat. Add salt to taste but remember that the sauce will slightly evaporate.

Simmer the meat for 1 ½ - 2 hours. The beef should be very soft.

Around 15 minutes before the end of simmering add a bay leaf to the **meat Hebrew-style**.

Hebrew-style meat is now ready. The pieces of meat are very tasty and soft and the sauce, resulting from the simmering, is very intense. All onions have melted adding a little thickness to the sauce.

Schnellklops

Schnellklops means "quick chop". It's a dish of Austrian and German cuisine.
Traditionally, **Schnellklops** is served with boiled or mashed potatoes but it's also perfect with pasta and rice, so there's no problem with choosing the appropriate garnish.
In this recipe **Schnellklops** is made from beef chunks.

To make Schnellklops you will need

For 2 servings.

Meat. 400 g. I am using a beef blade.
Onion. 1 medium bulb.
Sour cream. More than 20% fat. 2-3 tablespoons.
Flour. 2 tablespoons.
Salt. To taste.
Black pepper freshly ground. To taste.
Parsley. Several sprigs.
Vegetable oil. 2-3 tablespoons.

Cooking Schnellklops

Chop the meat into small pieces across the fibers.
Tenderize the meat slightly.
Heat vegetable oil in a deep frying pan.
Roll meat in flour and start to fry.
It's always better to fry the meat in parts to get crusty chops. Otherwise, the meat will lose the juice and will start to stew.
Fry on both sides until strong golden brown. No need to stir in the meantime - just wait until one side of the chops is fried, then flip and fry on the other side.
While the meat is roasting, dice the onion finely.

When the meat is browned, take it out of the pan, add a little vegetable oil, if necessary, and spread onions to the same pan.

Immediately sprinkle a little salt over the onion so it fries better and gives away more intense smell.

Fry the onion until transparent and light golden.

Finely chop the parsley, add a half to the onions and stir.

Add the meat to the fried onions and salt to taste.

Since we're using beef chops instead of minced meat for schnellklops, the dish should be stewed for about 30 minutes to be soft. Add a little boiling water just to partially cover the meat and cover the pan. Reduce the heat only to maintain boiling a little and you can forget about cooking for half an hour!

Dilute the sour cream with milk. And pour it to the stew.

Stir and add freshly ground black pepper.

Reduce the heat to low, to barely boiling.

Stew the meat in sour cream for at least 15 minutes, preferably 30 minutes. Cooking time actually depends on the cut of beef you are using. The tenderer the cut, the less time you need for stewing.

In the end the meat should be very soft and tender.

Schnellklops is traditionally served with boiled potatoes. Serve them with meat and sauce and sprinkle the dish with finely chopped parsley.

Tatar Azu

Azu is a dish of Tatar cuisine, which harmoniously combines cuts of meat and vegetables. Beef, lamb or horse-meat is most commonly used.

The choice of ingredients is very simple; the dish is easy to cook and gives a great taste experience.

Azu is a typical homemade dish, perfect to feed a large family thanks to its delectable taste and abundance.

For Azu you will need

Beef. 1 kg. Blade or neck are the best for **azu**.
Potatoes. 700 g.
Onion. 1 large bulb.
Pickles (without vinegar) 2-3 pcs.
Carrot. 1 pc.
Garlic. 2 cloves.
Fresh tomatoes (300 g).
Butter. 50-60 g.
Green onions. To taste.
Salt. To taste.
Black pepper freshly ground. To taste.
Bay leaf. 1-2 pcs.
A little vegetable oil for frying.

Cooking Azu

Dice the meat finely.

Heat the vegetable oil and about ⅓ (20 g) of butter in a very deep saute pan.

Fry the meat at high heat, stirring occasionally, until the juice evaporates.

While the meat is frying, cut onions into quarter-rings and the carrots into thin, medium-sized strips.

Add the onion and carrots to the meat and salt it lightly. Don't salt the meat too much at the beginning as there will be pickles added to the dish.

Sprinkle with freshly ground black pepper. Reduce the heat to medium and let it fry, stirring from time to time.

Cut pickles into strips.

Fry onions and carrots until the smell of fried onions. The onion will begin to become transparent and the carrot will limp slightly.

Add sliced cucumbers to the meat.

Mix everything again and let the pickles sizzle a little bit with the rest of the contents of the pan.

Remove the skins from the tomatoes – cut the skin, keep pouring boiling water over the tomatoes for a few minutes, then quickly drop them into cold water. Fresh tomatoes should be cut into small pieces.

Add tomatoes to the pan and stir. Let them warm up for a minute, and then add boiling water, so it covers the meat almost completely.

Bring the stew to a boil, and then reduce the heat, cover loosely to allow moisture to slowly boil away and stew for 1 hour.

About 40 minutes before the end of stewing time, process with the potatoes.

Peel them and cut into small dices of about 2 cm.

In a large and wide frying pan, heat vegetable oil and the remaining butter. The butter will give taste to the potatoes and vegetable oil will prevent from scorching.

Spread the chopped potatoes in hot oil, preferably in a single layer.

Don't stir for the first two or three minutes. Don't salt the potatoes either.

While the potatoes are frying, finely chop the garlic.

Most of the moisture from the saute pan with the meat has already evaporated. Add the garlic and stir.

Fry the potatoes on all sides until golden brown.

By the time the potatoes are ready, the meat has already stewed. Most of the moisture has evaporated, leaving some sauce, but the bottom of the pan is already visible when stirring.

Add fried potatoes to the pan.

Stir gently without breaking the potato pieces. Add 1-2 bay leaves.

Cover **azu** and let it sizzle at medium heat for about 10 minutes so that all the ingredients exchange their tastes and smells. Stir only once in the meantime.

Cut the greens.

Turn off the flame; keep **azu** covered for 5 minutes, then spread on plates, sprinkle with chopped greens and serve.

Shepherd's Pie

Shepherd's Pie is a classic English dish, also known as **Cottage pie**. The dish is simple and very home-style. It's very rich in taste, flavorful and convenient for serving.

To make Shepherd's Pie you will need

For meat filling

Chopped meat. Lamb or beef. 500 g.
Onion. 1 small bulb.
Leek. 1 small stalk. Only the white part.
Carrot. 1 pc.
Green peas. Fresh, frozen or canned. ~ 5 tablespoons.
Tomato paste. 2 tablespoons.
Dry red wine. 200 ml.
Black pepper freshly ground. To taste.
Salt. To taste.

For mashed potatoes

Potatoes. 700 g.
Milk or cream. 1 cup, depending on how the potatoes will absorb the liquid.
Butter. 50-80 g.
Salt. To taste.

For cake topping

Cheese. ~ 100 g.

Cooking Shepherd's Pie

Preparation of meat filling for cottage pie should be combined in time with preparation of the mashed potatoes.
Peel the potatoes, cut them into large chunks, bring salted water to a boil and let them cook until done.
At the same time move on to making the meat filling.
Cut the onions and carrots into small dices.
Heat vegetable oil in a deep frying pan at medium heat and fry the carrots for 2 minutes.
Then add the onions and a little salt stir and fry for a few minutes until the smell of fried onions.
Then add the minced meat.
Splitting large pieces of meat with a spatula, fry all together to the point where all the mince turns white and the golden crust just starts to appear.
While the meat is frying, cut leeks into medium-sized pieces and add them to the pan.
Stir. Let the leeks warm up for about 1 minute.
Move the filling on one half of the frying pan and spread the tomato paste on the other half.
Lightly fry the tomato paste, stirring constantly, to remove the characteristic smell and light acidity.
Mix the tomato paste with all contents of the pan, and add peas.
Stir everything again, add the dry red wine, salt and freshly ground black pepper. Stir again.
Bring the contents of the saucepan to a boil and turn the heat down to the minimum necessary to maintain a slight boil.
Stew until almost all the moisture has evaporated. Don't let it dry out but don't leave any liquid either.

Preparing mashed potatoes for the Shepherd's Pie.

Heat up the milk or cream but don't let it boil.
Drain cooked potatoes, add butter and hot milk. If you add cold milk to the potatoes, they might turn grey.
Mash the potatoes with a masher until completely smooth.
I strongly dissuade you from using a blender or a mixer as instead of delicate and fluffy potatoes you will get a gluey mass.

All you have to do now is put together the **Shepherd's Pie**.
Lightly grease the bottom and sides of the casserole with butter.
Lay all the meat filling at the bottom of the dish evenly.
Spread mashed potatoes on top.
Sprinkle with grated cheese.
Put the dish to a preheated 200ºC oven and cook until the cheese is completely melted and golden brown.
Serve hot.

Pork Stir Frying

Stir Frying is a cooking method in which all the products, pre-cut into thin slices, are quickly fried in hot oil while being stirred in a wok.
It's because this kind of cooking needs constant stirring that all the ingredients are prepared in advance, which is very characteristic for Chinese, or rather Cantonese cuisine, as there is no time to cut anything while cooking.

To make the Pork Stir Frying you will need

Pork. 300 g. Pork neck would be the best.
Soy sauce. 70-80 ml. + some for marinating.
Ginger. A small piece of 2-3 cm.
Garlic. 1 clove + 1 clove for marinating.
Onion. 1 bulb.
Carrot. 1 pc.
Celery. 1 stalk.
Bulgarian pepper. 1 pc.
Green onion. 1 stalk.
If desired and if near at hand, you can enlarge the list of ingredients by adding: mushrooms (Chinese wood, shiitake, white mushrooms), shredded cabbage, pineapple, green radish, eggplant, radish, cucumber, etc.

Preparing products for the Pork Stir Frying

It's perfect if you can marinate the pork the day before. Cut the pork into small pieces 2-3 cm thick and marinate in a mixture of soy sauce, water, and garlic (one clove).

If you need to cook quickly, just chop the pork into thin strips and marinate it in the same marinade for about 20-30 minutes.

Slice the onion into thin half-rings, the white part of green onions into pieces 3 cm each. Cut the carrot into thin strips the size of a match. Cut the celery thinly and diagonally and cut the Bulgarian pepper into strips.

If you use any additional ingredients, also cut them in this way - the mushrooms are cut into thin slices.

Clean the ginger and cut in round pieces.

Cut the second clove into large slices.

The ginger and garlic are used only for flavoring oil, not for food anyway.

Cooking the Pork Stir Frying

It's best to cook in a wok but a deep frying pan can also be used.

Warm the oil at high heat.

Put the onion, carrot and celery.

Stirring constantly, fry the vegetables quickly, for just a minute or a minute and a half, until they start to become tender, then add chopped green onion - the white part - and pepper.

Tossing constantly, fry everything together for as long as the pepper starts to become tender.

If you use more ingredients, add them as well. If there are too many vegetables, cook them partially.

The main rule is not to overdo, the vegetables should remain slightly crispy in the middle.

Move the vegetables from the pan into a bowl and proceed with frying the meat.

If necessary, add the oil and heat it up again to a high temperature.

Throw the chopped ginger and garlic to hot oil and fry for 30 seconds, but don't let it burn.

Then add the pork must be very hot, almost sizzling, for the pork to begin to caramelize quickly.

Stir and fry the pork until done.

It's important not to have raw meat inside but at the same time not to let it dry while frying too long.

When the pork is fried add the soy sauce.

Constantly tossing, bring the sauce to a boil - it will take 10-20 seconds, then evaporate it slightly, frying for about a minute, remove the garlic and ginger, they've done their job, and add roasted vegetables and almost all the chopped green onions, the green part.

Again, stir all together so the sauce covers each piece.

As an option, you can add a teaspoon of starch diluted with cold water. It will slightly thicken the sauce and obtain an outside gloss.

21

Pork stir frying tastes best with bland rice or noodles. Put the pan contents on a plate, spread rice around, sprinkle with remaining green onions and serve immediately on the table.

Falscher Hase

Falscher Hase is a German dish, or I should say a Prussian one to be more specific, with its roots up to the second half of the 18th century and it's a **meat casserole** with a variety of fillings.

Because only the aristocracy had the right to hunt and thus use game as food, the representatives of the third and fourth classes didn't see any hunted goodies on their tables.

The name "**Falscher Hase**", which literally means "False Hare", is therefore ironic because the hare had never been present in a traditional cuisine of the poorest Prussians. Yet, the dish was invented.

The dish is quite simple to prepare, but at the same time very tasty, served both hot as the main dish and cold as an entree or the main ingredient of a sandwich.

The term "false hare" also is extremely suitable in this recipe as the only essential ingredient of the filling is hard-boiled eggs.

To make the False Hare you will need

Chopped meat. 700 g. Beef and pork 50/50.
Onion. 2 large bulbs.
Carrot. 1 pcs.
Bulgarian pepper. ½-1 pc.
Celery. 1 stalk.
Eggs. 4 pcs.
Garlic. 1 clove.
White dried bread, 3-4 slices.
A small bunch of dill.
Sour cream. 50-70 ml.
Salt. To taste.
Black pepper freshly ground. To taste.
Vegetable oil for frying.

Cooking the False Hare

Hard-boil 3 eggs.
Soak slices of dried bread in water.
Dice finely all the vegetables - onions, celery, carrots and Bulgarian pepper.
Heat the oil in a frying pan and add the onion, carrot and celery. Season with a little salt. You can add a little pinch of sugar to enhance the taste and smell but also to make the onion fry better.
Stir and leave to brown at medium heat until the vegetables start to become tender.
Finely chop the garlic.
Add garlic and Bulgarian pepper to the pan to soften the vegetables.
Stir and fry all together.
In a deep bowl mix the minced meat, fried vegetables, bread (drained of excess moisture), a raw egg, salt and freshly ground black pepper.
Mix it all thoroughly to a smooth mince.
Preheat the oven to 180ºC-190ºC.
Take a large sheet of foil and fold it in half.
Spread about ⅓ of mince on the foil to obtain a rectangle 3 cm thick.
Make a layer of hard-boiled eggs. They can be cut lengthwise into halves - I think they will look better that way in the finished dish.
Cover the eggs with the remaining meat, forming a flat meat loaf.

Tightly wrap the loaf in foil, trying to make it as airtight as possible. If necessary, you can take another sheet of foil.

Place the loaf in a casserole and cook it in the oven for about 1h 20.

While the fake rabbit is being cooked, chop the dill.

Mix the chopped dill with sour cream.

When the casserole is ready, cut the foil and glaze the meat with sour cream and dill.

Cook for another 10 minutes to clot the cream.

Take the pan out from the oven and leave to rest for 10-15 minutes.

Chop the fake rabbit into pieces and serve with fresh vegetables or with your favorite garnish.

Cold dish tastes good as a snack or in sandwiches; the main rule is to slice it finely.

Cheese Sauce with Minced Meat

This **cheese sauce** is very similar to Mexican chile con queso, but it's richer in flavor and the presence of minced meat makes additional difference in taste.

This dish goes very well with pasta, so you don't have to keep this recipe for a special occasion, especially with the express preparation time of only 30 minutes!

To make Cheese Sauce with Minced Meat you will need

Portion: Approximately 400 ml of a ready sauce.

Minced meat 500 g. Beef and pork 1:1 mix is the best.
Onion. 1 medium bulb.
Hot peppers. 1 pc.
A medium tomato.
Garlic. 1 clove.
Cheese. 1 package.
Milk. 400 ml.
A mixture of Mexican spices.
Salt. To taste.
Freshly ground black pepper. To taste.

Cooking Cheese Sauce with Minced Meat

Finely chop the onions and hot peppers. The amount depends on the desired spiciness of the pepper sauce.
Dice the garlic.

Heat up a little vegetable oil in a saucepan at medium heat and add diced onions and hot peppers.

Fry a few minutes until onion is transparent, then add garlic and Mexican spices.

Stir and let the garlic and spices warm up and slightly brown.

Quickly chop tomatoes into small pieces.

Add the tomatoes, stir and simmer a little in their juice.

Then add the minced meat.

Mash large pieces of minced into really small ones with a spatula and fry until slight crispy crust.

Pour the milk, add salt and freshly ground black pepper.

Wait for the milk to come to a boil and add grated cheese.

Stir until completely dissolved, turn the heat down and let the sauce boil for a bit.

Wait until the sauce begins to thicken and turn off the heat.

Pour hot sauce into a gravy boat and serve with nachos, chips or pasta.

Vegetable Stew with Meat

Vegetable stew with meat must be quite popular worldwide thanks to commonly used ingredients and a full flavor.

To make Vegetable Stew with Meat you will need

Meat. 700 g. Beef brisket suits best.
Eggplant. 1 pc.
Zucchini. 1 pc.
Carrot. 3-4 medium pcs.
Potatoes. 4 medium pcs.
Onion. 2 medium bulbs.
Tomatoes. 150-200 g.
Garlic. 1-2 cloves.
Salt. To taste.
Freshly ground black pepper. To taste.
Vegetable oil, 30-50 ml.

Cooking Vegetable Stew with Beef

Dice the meat. The beef with a small amount of fat is far the best.
Dice the onion and carrot.
Heat up vegetable oil in a deep saucepan and fry the meat.
The meat will at first give away a certain amount of juice. Fry the meat at high heat, stirring it until the moisture has evaporated and the meat pieces have been covered with a golden fried crust.
Then add the onion.
Stir again, reduce the heat to medium, wait until the onion starts to become transparent and add the carrots.
Then stir again and fry all together until the carrot softens and vegetables fry.
Add a bit of boiling water, so that the meat is covered by about ⅔ and stew the dish covered at medium heat for about 30 minutes.
During this time, you will have just enough time to peel and chop the potatoes into small pieces.
In 30 minutes add potatoes to the saucepan. Stir again and cover the pan.
Dice the zucchini. If it's quite young, peeling and removing seeds isn't necessary.
Chop the eggplant as well. Again, peeling it or not is up to you. Remember that peeled eggplant quickly loses its shape and blends in the sauce.

Slice the garlic.

Add zucchini, garlic, eggplant, salt and pepper to the saucepan.

Cover the pan, dice the tomatoes and add them to the stew.

Stew at medium heat until cooked. It takes another 15 minutes.

Turn off the heat and let the **vegetable stew with meat** infuse for at least 5 minutes.

After, spread the stew on plates, sprinkle with finely chopped greens and enjoy your meal.

Porchetta

Porchetta is a traditional **Italian dish** – it's a roasted pork roll, always with a delicious crispy skin.

Porchetta tastes divine both hot and cold, so this dish can be served as a main dish or a snack.

To make Porchetta you will need

A piece of pork peritoneum, always with the skin.

Pork tenderloin.

Lemon.

Garlic. 8-10 cloves.

Rosemary.

Thyme.

Fennel seeds.

Chile. Flakes.

Salt. To taste.

Black pepper freshly ground. To taste.

The amount of products isn't indicated deliberately. Choose according to your own appetite.

Cooking Porchetta

The most important thing is to choose the right meat for porchetta.

Two cuts of meat are used the most frequently - pork tenderloin and pork peritoneum, always with the skin.

Remember that the tenderloin will be wrapped in the piece of peritoneum, so the latter should big enough to completely wrap the tenderloin and still have a small margin of 3-5 cm left.

Choose a cut of the peritoneum with the maximum amount of meat and a little fat.

Wash the piece of peritoneum; scrape the skin with a knife to complete cleanness.

Put the peritoneum skin down, try on the tenderloin on it.

Try to wrap the peritoneum around the tenderloin. If there is a margin, mark the spot where the tenderloin ends.

Expand the peritoneum and make an incision like you wanted to cut away this "extra" piece of meat, but the incision shouldn't be too deep – only to cut the meat, not the skin, as this piece of skin will overlap on the roll and thus will wrap it better.

Chop the garlic but don't dice it.

Wash the lemon, pour boiling water over it to enhance the flavor, and grate the lemon zest on a fine grater, using the yellow part of the peel only. One lemon zest is enough.

Put the piece of peritoneum on a cutting board skin down and cut the meat crosswise, diamond-shape. The main thing is not to cut the meat through the skin. The cut should end about 0.5-1 cm from the skin.

Evenly salt the pork, and then evenly spread the garlic with lemon zest. Sprinkle herbs - rosemary, thyme and fennel seeds. If using dried herbs, just gently rub them with your fingers. Season the meat with chili flakes and black pepper as well.

Rub the garlic, salt, herbs and spices over the meat cuts.

Turn a tight roll from the peritoneum with tenderloin inside.

Bind the roll with a string to fix its shape.

Tightly wrap the prepared **porchetta** in baking paper so the skin doesn't burn nor stick to the foil while roasting.

Then wrap the porchetta in a double layer of foil and put to the fridge for a day, for the meat to be marinated in garlic and spices.

The next day, roast **Porchetta** in an oven preheated to 150°C -160°C for 3 hours.

Take it out of the oven and remove the paper and foil it was wrapped in, then place the meat on a new sheet of baking paper. Increase the oven temperature to 200°C and roast the meat until the skin has been caramelized and crispy. The main thing is to keep a close eye on the meat and often flip the porchetta so the skin becomes roasted evenly and crispy across the surface of the roll.

Once the skin is nicely roasted, take **Porchetta** out from the oven and give it 10 minutes to cool down.

Afterwards, remove the string, cut **Porchetta** into portions and serve.

Pork with Gooseberry Sauce

Pork with gooseberry sauce has pleasantly surprised me by its flavor. When I started to cook it for the first time, I couldn't quite imagine how the sauce would taste.

Sweet and sour cream sauce remarkably emphasizes the taste of pork and green onions greatly enrich the flavor of the sauce and meat.

To make Pork with Gooseberry Sauce you will need

Pork tenderloin. 400-450 g.
Gooseberry. 1 cup.
Sweet Cream. 200 ml.
Sugar. 1-2 tablespoons, depending on the degree of gooseberry acidity.
Flour. 1 tablespoon with a heap.
Green onions. 8 large sprigs.
Dill. Several sprigs.
Parsley. Several sprigs.
Salt. To taste.
Freshly ground black pepper. To taste.

Cooking Pork with Gooseberry Sauce

Chop the pork into pieces 2-2.5 cm thick.
Season the meat with salt and pepper to taste.
Preheat vegetable oil in a large frying pan. Medium heat should be good.
Roll the pieces of meat in flour and put them to the pan.
Fry for 4 minutes on each side until golden brown.
Then, leave it to cool.

Making Gooseberry Sauce

While preparing the sauce, heat up the oven to 180° C.
Wash the berries and cut off the stalk and the remnants of flowers.
Cut the berries in halves.
In a small pot, mix berries with sugar and a tablespoon of water.
Put the bucket on a cooker and bring it a boil.
Cook for about 5 minutes.
Then turn the heat down a little and pour cream in the gooseberry. Immediately stir and bring to a boil again.
Cook for 2 minutes at a very low heat and turn off the heat when done.
In a casserole, spread the pork and generously sprinkle it with chopped green onion, leaving a little onion for sprinkling the top of the pork.
Pour creamy gooseberry sauce over the pork.
Sprinkle with chopped herbs.
With a fork, slightly press the herbs so they sink in the sauce.
Roast for 30-40 minutes. Time can vary depending on the amount of meat and sauce.
Prepare the plates, sprinkle just a bit of fresh herbs, spread the meat and serve very hot.

Adobo

Adobo is a Filipino dish.
Adobo can be made of red meat, poultry, seafood, vegetables – almost everything fits! Just like any home-made dish, Adobo doesn't have anyone generally accepted recipe, so it allows you to experiment and cook according to your preferences.
Pork is used in my recipe.

To make Adobo you will need

Pork. 700 g.
Onion. 2 medium bulbs.
Garlic. 5-6 cloves.
Soy sauce. ~ 100 ml.
Vinegar. ~ 2 tablespoons. Best of all is a fine 6% grape vinegar as it will be tenderer and richer in taste than the non-brewed condiment.
Sugar. 1-2 teaspoon.
Black pepper freshly ground.
Red hot pepper.
Bay leaf. 2-3 pcs.

Cooking Adobo

Dice the meat into the "one-bite" pieces.
Slice the onions into lengthwise but not too thin - 3-5 millimeters thick. Don't chop garlic very finely either.
In a saucepan, heat up vegetable oil and add the pork.

Fry the pork to the evaporation of the liquid and until a light crust.

Spread chopped onions and garlic to the pork.

Add the red pepper to taste, so that it enhances the flavor of meat and onions.

Stir and fry at medium heat until the onion has been transparent. Frying takes 5-7 minutes. High heat is redundant as it would burn the onions and garlic.

While the onions are frying, mix soy sauce, vinegar, sugar and water in a bowl/cup. I usually take about as much water as the soy sauce. If you add only the soy sauce, without dilution with water, then you risk getting a very salty dish.

Stir it all and taste the mixture to get a sour-sweet-salty flavor, based on your taste preferences.

Add the black pepper freshly ground to additionally flavor the marinade.

Add the marinade and a bay leaf to the stewing meat.

The amount of marinade should be just enough to keep the meat stewing.

Close the lid, reduce the heat to a little below medium and stew until fully cooked.

For pork, it will take 40-60 minutes.

Adobo is traditionally served with rice.

The dish is very tasty, fragrant and bright. And quite simple to make as you can see!

Viennese Schnitzel

Traditional Viennese schnitzel is made from veal. Thin chops, in a golden crispy breading, it's soft and tender.

You should know that a typical Viennese schnitzel is very large – it's sticking out from a plate!

In my recipe, **Viennese schnitzel** isn't planned to be this big, but apart from the size, all the other principles of a traditional recipe were kept, including serving on the table.

To make the Viennese Schnitzel you will need

Veal.
Milk.
Egg.
Flour.

Vegetable oil.
<u>Fresh</u> white bread.
Salt.
Butter for the final roasting.

The amount of products isn't indicated deliberately. Choose according to your own appetite.

Cooking the Viennese Schnitzel

Slice veal finely, the chops should be thinner than 1 cm.
Tenderize the meat with a flat hammer. The thickness of the piece shouldn't exceed 4 mm.
Cut away the crust of the fresh white bread; cut the crumb into small pieces and put it to the blender cup.
Mill the bread into crumbs.
What's important is that only fresh bread crumbs can be used to make a perfect Viennese schnitzel. Traditional breadcrumbs won't give the same flavor results as only fresh bread guarantees crunchy and delicate breading.
In a large bowl, break eggs – 1 egg for 2 very large schnitzels. Add milk – the same volume as the egg, season with salt and add a little vegetable oil.
Mix thoroughly.
In a large thick-walled pan, heat up a sufficiently thick - about 5-7 mm - layer of vegetable oil. Oil should be hot, but not sizzling for the breading to roast, but not immediately burn.
Now, it's time to dip the chops in the breading: roll the tenderized schnitzel in flour, shaking off the excess of flour, dip it on both sides in the egg mixture and, having allowed the surplus egg to drain, smother it in bread crumbs.
Breading should be sufficiently solid, but not thick.
Lay the schnitzel in the hot oil and fry for 2-3 minutes on each side. Since the schnitzel is very thin, frying will be very quick.
When all the schnitzels are already browned, pour the vegetable oil out of the pan, wipe the pan with a paper towel and melt the butter in it.
Fry the schnitzels in butter very quickly, just for 30-40 seconds on each side, and then put them on paper towels to get rid of excess oil and butter.

Gently sprinkle schnitzel with lemon juice on a plate.

Beef a la Chinese

As usual in China, meat is cooked very quickly. Spicy and juicy, it's excellent for both a usual family meals and for a party.

You can serve it with any garnish or simply with sliced vegetables.

To make Beef a la Chinese you will need

Beef. Steak or tenderloin is best.
Soy sauce.
Garlic.
Ginger.
Black pepper freshly ground.
Chili. Fresh or dried or flakes – doesn't matter.
Sesame.
Vegetable oil.

The amount of products isn't indicated deliberately. Choose according to your own appetite.

Cooking Beef a la Chinese

Chop the meat into thin strips about 5 centimeters long.

Chop garlic and fresh or dry chili not very finely. We will use it partially to marinate the meat and partially to flavor the oil. The amount you use depends on how spicy you want the dish to be.

Put meat, half of garlic and chili to a bowl and add a bit of ginger and soy sauce.

Mix it all thoroughly and leave for at least 20-30 minutes to marinate.

When the meat is being marinated, heat up vegetable oil to a high temperature in a frying pan. Then fry the remaining garlic and hot pepper in this oil very quickly.

Remove the garlic and pepper from the oil, it has already flavored the oil, and the further frying would only make it taste bitter.

Fry the pieces of meat in small batches just for a few minutes in very hot oil. At first, they might be a lot of juice as the marinade, which was absorbed by the meat, will start to boil. Therefore, you need to instantly vaporize the marinade for the meat to fry.

Stir and fry the meat until a delicate crust – don't fry it too long not to dry it out.

The beef a la Chinese is ready. Sprinkle it with sesame seeds roasted in a dry frying pan with no additional oil. Don't roast them too long, otherwise they will taste bitter.

Garnish - any or none at all. Traditionally, you can serve rice, fried noodles and vegetables both fresh and fried.

You get a spicy, tasty and very soft meat, if not dry and over fried.

Meat in Soy Sauce

Soy sauce is a perfect base for marinades and it goes well with almost any red meat and poultry. Its preparation methods can also be quite various.

In this recipe, we make beef in sauce a la Chinese. It is cooked quickly, but you need at least half an hour for the beef to get marinated.

For Meet in Soy Sauce you will need

About 2-3 servings.

Beef. 300-400 g.
Soy sauce. 100 ml.
Starch. About 2 tablespoons.
Bulgarian pepper. 1 pcs.
Onion. 1-2 bulbs.
Hot peppers. Fresh or dry.
Garlic. 3 cloves.
Sugar. 1 teaspoon.
Black pepper freshly ground. To taste.

Cooking Meat in Soy Sauce

Cut the beef into thin strips.
Chop all the vegetables:
Chop Bulgarian pepper into small pieces; slice the onion lengthwise or in semi-rings. Remove seeds and white fibers from the hot peppers chop the peppers finely. Slice 2 cloves of garlic.
Put the meat in a small saucepan or a bowl, pour a mix of soy sauce and water 2:1, so it's not too salty. Add sugar, starch, a clove of garlic crushed with the flat side of the knife blade and a portion of chopped ginger. If you want to, add freshly ground black pepper.
Mix it all well and leave for at least 30 minutes to marinate.
The meat is sliced very thinly, so it marinates quickly and after about half an hour you can begin to cook.
Preheat 2 tablespoons of vegetable oil in a frying pan.
First quickly fry the onion. Once the onion softens a bit, add chopped hot pepper and garlic. Fry for a minute.
Add Bulgarian pepper and fry all together for a minute and a half, stirring.
Cover the pan to keep the vegetables warm.
Take another pan, add a tablespoon of vegetable oil and heat it up. Take the meat out of the marinade and fry. Don't drain the marinade; it will serve as the basis for the sauce. Quickly fry the meat pieces until slight fried crust. The heat must be high and the oil hot, so the remaining marinade evaporates fast and the meat is fried, not stewed. Frying takes about 3 minutes.
Add the vegetables to the meat and stir.
Add the marinade to the pan, about a little more than half a glass. Bring the marinade to a boil; it will thicken thanks to the starch.
 Turn off the heat. Beef in soy sauce is ready.
 The dish is served well with rice or fried noodles.

Navy-Style Macaroni

Navy-style macaroni is a wonderful souvenir from my childhood, very classic, delicious and easy to make. The ingredients are simple and available.

Meat cooked in water or broth is typically used for this dish. Since this kind of meat isn't eaten very often, especially by the children, we need a recipe that allows us to use this meat to make a quick and tasty dish.

For Navy-Style Macaroni you will need

Cooked meat. Beef is the most commonly used. 150 g.
Macaroni. The amount is up to you.
Onion. A small bulb.
Salt to taste.
Freshly ground black pepper to taste.
Butter for frying.

The amount of products isn't indicated deliberately. Choose according to your own appetite.

Cooking Navy-Style Macaroni

Grind the meat with a blender.
Dice the onion finely.
Cooking meat and macaroni will be parallel as the time it takes to prepare the beef will be just enough for cooking macaroni.
Boil a pot of water, salt it, and put macaroni in the boiling water. Cook them until ready as written on the package.
Preheat a lot of butter in a frying pan because the minced meat will absorb a lot of it.
Fry the onion until strong smell and the color changes to golden.
Spread the minced meat on roasted onions, stir and let the mince fry a bit. Add salt and freshly ground black pepper to taste.
When the beef is fried and pasta cooked, drain the pasta and immediately mix it with roasted meat.
Spread on a plate and serve on the table.

Pork Chop Stuffed with Apples

Pork chops and apples - What a wonderful combination!

To make Pork Chop Stuffed with Apples you will need

Pork chopped into thick chops.
Sour-sweet apple.
Breadcrumbs. About 1 tablespoon on each two chops.
Thyme and rosemary. Choose herbs according to your taste. There are no strict recommendations for spices in this recipe.
Freshly ground black pepper.

The amount of products isn't indicated deliberately. Choose according to your own appetite.

Cooking Pork Chops Stuffed with Apples

Clean the thyme and rosemary leaves from the stems.
Throw the stems of thyme away. You can leave the stems of rosemary aside, if they are solid enough. Chop the leaves finely.
Peel the apple, cut the seed box off and grate on a coarse grater.
Mix the grated apple, almost all the chopped herbs, breadcrumbs, freshly ground black pepper and a little salt in a suitable deep bowl.
During preparation the crumbs will absorb the moisture from the apples and the stuffing won't be loose or watery.
Tenderize the chops gently, don't use too much force nor a hammer with teeth - the surface of the meat should remain intact, without punctures.
The chops should be thick half a centimeter or two. Make a quite big "pocket" on the side for the stuffing. The most convenient way to do it is to use a small sharp knife and try to make a teardrop-shaped cut, with the narrow part being the place where the knife went into the meat.
At the same time, do not to cut through the piece – leave about 1 centimeter to the edge so the stuffing doesn't leak out.
Stuff the meat with the apple stuffing quite tight. Then clip the cut with a wooden toothpick or sew it up. You can use the rosemary stems you saved.
Season the chops with salt on all sides and rub gently black pepper and herbs: thyme and rosemary.
Fry them on both sides in a well-heated frying pan with a small amount of vegetable oil until golden brown. Do it in parts, without letting the pan cool down with too much meat in it. We want the chops to roast, not stew.
Spread the fried pieces of meat on a baking paper and roast in the oven preheated to 180°C.
Keep the meat in the oven until cooked. Check the readiness by making a puncture in the thickest part of the meat. If the clear, colorless juice appears, the meat is ready. If the juice is bloody or even slightly pink, keep the meat in the oven for a little while.
Serve the chops stuffed with apples hot. Almost any garnish or a salad will be suitable.

Pork Chops in Maple Syrup

It's commonly known that pork tastes wonderful accompanied by sweet-sour or sweet sauces or marinades. That's why honey, sugar or all kinds of sweet syrups are often used as the main ingredients of pork marinade's and sauces.
Obviously it couldn't have been different with this recipe in which we will use sweet marinade and glaze, with maple syrup as a leading flavor. Moreover, you can prepare the meat in the oven or in the barbecue.

For the Pork Chops in Maple Syrup you will need

Pork chop 2-3 cm thick.

Maple syrup.

Grape or apple vinegar 5-6%. In the ratio approximately ¼-⅓ of the amount of syrup.

Garlic. Several cloves.

Salt. To taste.

Black pepper freshly ground pepper or mixed peppercorns.

To prepare 1 chop, take approximately 50 ml of maple syrup and 15 ml of 5% of wine vinegar.

Cooking Pork Chops in Maple Syrup

First, we need to prepare the marinade for pork which will also be used as a glaze when cooking.

Grate the garlic on a fine grater or use a garlic press. Try to squeeze the maximum of the garlic juice to the marinade.

In a bowl, mix maple syrup, vinegar and grated garlic. Add freshly ground pepper.

Glaze pork chops with ¼ of the marinade and leave to pickle for at least 30 minutes, the longer the better. We'll use the rest to glaze the meat when roasting. It's best to use a silicone brush for thin layers.

Take out the meat, salt it on both sides and spread on a baking pan covered with baking paper. Unlike foil, baking paper doesn't stick that much to the meat. Spread a thin layer of glaze on the chops.

Put the meat to a preheated 220° C oven and roast for about 10 minutes.

Then reduce the oven temperature to 190° C - 180° C and re-glaze the meat.

Cook until the meat is done - it should take 20-25 minutes, depending on the oven and the thickness of the chops. Glaze the meat every 3-5 minutes.

It's best to glaze the chops more often with a thin layer rather than dipping the meat in the marinade only once as a thick glaze layer will cool the surface of the meat and the moisture from the glaze will be boiling and evaporating for a long time making the meat be boil, not roast.

Check the readiness of the chops - pierce the thickest point of the chop with a toothpick or a thin knife. If the meat juice is transparent, the meat is ready.

Get the chops from the oven and serve. Fresh vegetables, French fries or roasted potatoes will suit very well as garnish.

This recipe is also great for the barbecue - surprise your guests by preparing grilled chops.

Moussaka

Moussaka is a Greek dish and it's a casserole of eggplants, minced meat and potatoes.

Preparation of moussaka does take some time but it's still worth the effort. The dish is very rich but at the same time not too stodgy. This quality food is appropriate not only for everyday meals but it will also take a rightful place among the dishes, you'll serve to your guests on a festive day.

To make Moussaka you will need

4 small eggplants.

Potatoes. 4 medium-sized bulbs.

Chopped meat. 500 g. Beef and pork, ratio 1:1.

Tomatoes. 300-400 g.

Onion. 1 bulb.

Garlic. 2-3 cloves.

Parsley. 1 bunch.

Wine. White dry. 100 ml.

Vegetable oil.

Salt. To taste.

Black pepper freshly ground. To taste.

The amount of products is just enough for you to fill out a 25x18x6 cm form completely.

And for the sauce you will need:
Milk. 500 ml.
Egg. 2 pcs.
Flour. 2 tablespoons with a heap.
Butter. 70-100 g.
Parmesan cheese. 50-60 g.
Salt. To taste.

Cooking Moussaka

Once again, I would like to warn that the dish requires sufficient time, effort and attention. If possible, sauce and stuffing should be prepared the day before.

Stage 1 - Preparing the stuffing for Moussaka

Dice the onion finely.
Preheat vegetable oil in a saucepan and fry the onion at a sufficiently high heat until golden.
Add the mince to the onion and fry, mashing large pieces with a spatula.
Cut the eggplants lengthwise into rings of about 5 mm thick, season with salt and place in a colander for the emerging moisture to drain easily.
Dice the garlic finely, don't use a garlic press.
The minced meat in the saucepan will first give the juice to be evaporated by stirring and frying. As soon as the meat juice evaporates and the meat begins to fry, add the garlic and salt.
Pour 100 ml of dry white wine, stir and let the wine evaporate.
Dice the tomatoes. You can first remove the skin from them but I don't.
Add tomatoes to the stuffing.
Stir and reduce the heat.

Chop the parsley – leaves only.

Add parsley to the pan and stir again.

Let it stew for 30 minutes. The goal is to let the mince stew in tomato juice, evaporating the maximum amount of moisture along the way.

To make perfect moussaka, cooked mince should be rather dry.

Stage 2 - Making a sauce for Moussaka

While the meat sauce is stewing, grate 50-60 grams of Parmesan cheese on a fine grater.

Preheat a little butter in a saucepan and add the flour into it. Constantly stir until flour starts to change color. Gradually pour the milk and keep on stirring to avoid lumps and obtain a smooth mass. Add a little salt, depending on how salty Parmesan is. Constantly stirring, cook the sauce at low heat to thicken.

Then turn off the heat and add all the grated cheese. Stir vigorously to let the cheese melt and be evenly distributed in the sauce.

Give the sauce about 5 minutes to cool and add 2 eggs. If you add the eggs to the boiling sauce, they will curdle immediately and we definitely don't want that.

Again, stir it all carefully until completely smooth. The sauce is ready.

By the time you finish, the meat sauce should be ready as well - it shouldn't have the excess moisture anymore.

Stage 3 - Preparation of the moussaka vegetable component

Preheat vegetable oil in a large frying pan. Drain moisture from the eggplants with a paper towel and fry until light golden brown.

Spread fried eggplants on a paper towels to let the excess oil sink in.

Slice potatoes into rings, 5 mm thick, like the eggplants. Fry potatoes in hot oil until golden brown.

Spread potato slices on a paper towel too.

Stage 4 — Laying-out and cooking

The laying-out order:

Each layer should completely cover the entire area of the casserole. Therefore, when calculating the proportions of the ingredients, keep in mind that there will be at least 2 layers of each vegetable.

The height of my dish allows me to make only 6 layers so the description is exactly for this amount.
• The first layer - half of fried potatoes.
• The second layer - half of fried eggplants.
• The third layer - all the meat sauce.
• The fourth layer - the second half of the potatoes.
• The fifth layer - the second half of the eggplants.
• The sixth layer - all the cheese sauce.

As soon as you finish composing all the layers, leave the casserole for 5 minutes to let the sauce get inside the pie.

Then put the dish to a preheated 180°C oven and cook for about 30 minutes. If you want to, you can sprinkle grated cheese on top of moussaka 10 minutes before the time is up.

The dish is delicious both hot and cold.

Stuffed Pepper

Bulgarian pepper is probably one of the easiest vegetables to stuff. There are lots of stuffing possibilities, but minced meat with rice has definitely the garland of popularity. It's also going to be used in my recipe.

For Stuffed Peppers you will need

Proportions for 8 peppers.

Bulgarian pepper. 8 pcs.
Beef. Approximately 700 g.
Onion. 3-4 large bulbs.
2-3 medium carrots.
Rice. ½-⅔ of a cup.
Tomatoes. 700 grams or more.
Garlic. Optional. One clove in total or 1 clove per pepper.
Salt and freshly ground black pepper.
Vegetable oil.

Cooking Stuffed Peppers

First of all, cook the rice. Wash the rice several times and place it in the pot adding twice as much water as rice. Add some salt and bring to a boil at high heat, then reduce the heat and cover the pot.
When the rice absorbs all the water, taste it. If it's tender, leave it to cool without cover. Excessive moisture in the stuffing is completely unnecessary.
While the rice is being cooked, move on to preparing meat.
Slice part of the onions in rings and grind it in a blender.
Chop the meat into small pieces and grind it with the onions until smooth. Add salt and pepper to taste.
Move the meat to the bowl and mix it with the chilled rice.
Foil the bowl and put it to the fridge.
Slice the onion in quarter-rings and grate the carrots on a coarse grater.
Heat vegetable oil in a broad and deep saucepan and fry the onions and carrots. Add some salt to make the onion fry better, stir and leave at low heat to fry.
Dice the tomatoes into small pieces.
As soon as the vegetables soften and the onions start to become transparent, add the chopped tomatoes.
Stir the vegetables and let them fry / stew in their own juice.
While the basis for the sauce is being prepared, deal with the pepper.
Carefully cut out the stalk, take out the seeds and white fibers. You can simply to cut the stalk around with a small knife and push it inside the pepper. It will go off along with most of the seeds. Then, just take it out from the pepper.

Another way to clean the pepper is to cut off its cap – it's easier to clean, of course, but less convenient when you want to put it on a plate as well as while cooking as the caps tend to move or fall down. Personally, I'd rather cut out the stalk.

Take the stuffing out of the fridge and stuff the peppers very tightly.

By the time you finished, all the vegetables in the saucepan have stewed, so the basis for the sauce is ready. Place the peppers in the saucepan, spreading the sauce a little so that it gets between the peppers, not under them. Top up with boiling water to half the peppers. Add a little salt.

Tightly cover the saucepan and simmer at low heat until cooked. It will take about 40 minutes.

Beef Stew

What a comfortable dish! Make a large saucepan of a beef stew and be relaxed. Almost any garnish is good and the meat doesn't lose its flavor after re-heating. Beef stew is also a wonderful dish for children – very tender and delicate.

Even though it seems to be one of the easiest recipes for beef, it has an exceptional flavor.

To make Beef Stew you will need

Beef. 1½ kg.
Onion. 3 medium bulbs and more.
Salt. To taste.
Black peppercorns. 10-30 corns, depending on your personal preferences. For children, you can reduce the amount of pepper to 1-2 corns but even many black peppercorns won't add much spiciness.
Vegetable oil. 50-60 ml.
Water. Approximately 1½ cup.

Cooking Beef Stew

Meat from the leg is best for stewing.

This part of the carcass has a lot of connective tissue that reacts perfectly when stewing, softening the meat, not letting it become rigid and dry, and at the same time greatly enriches the sauce.

When it comes to the preparation, it's best to chop everything at once, so you don't get torn between the frying pan and the cutting board.

Chop the beef into small pieces.

Slice the onions. I cut onions in two ways. Half of the onions are sliced lengthwise so it gets completely dissolved and goes into the sauce while stewing.

The other half is cut in half or a quarter-rings so the pieces stay in the sauce as a whole.

Put the sliced meat on a dry, oil-free, well-heated frying pan.

The juice will come out.

Wait until all the moisture boils out and begins to brown.

Then pour the oil into the meat and stir well.

After 30 seconds the oil will heat up, fry the meat in the oil.

Add all onion at once and the black peppercorn. Season with salt.

Toss well for to the onions to get its portion of oil.

Let the onions fry with the meat.

Then, pour boiling water over the meat, covering it almost completely. Stir once again. Wait a second until the water boils.

Turn down the heat to low and cover the pan very tight.

Simmer the meat for two hours or two and a half at low heat.

Serve with any garnish, spreading the sauce heavily.

Ossobuco

Ossobuco is a traditional Italian dish. It's literally translated as an "empty bone" as the pieces of beef shank used for **ossobuco**, is sliced crosswise, including a bone, into thick hunks.

The preparation takes a lot of time as the meat needs to stew at least 2-3 hours, although while stewing it doesn't need any attention.

A very tasty and flavorful sauce is perfect both for meat and garnish. Although, **ossobuco** is traditionally served with Milanese risotto, it's no worse with pasta, potatoes or rice.

To make Ossobuco you will need

Beef shank, sliced crosswise into thick pieces of 4-5 cm thick together with the bone, about 1 kg.

1 small carrot.
2 small onion bulbs.
Tomatoes. 500 g.
Garlic. 2 cloves.
Celery. 1 stalk.
Wine. Dry white. 100 ml.
Bouillon. Beef or chicken. 500 ml.
Flour. 2 tablespoons.
Parsley. 2-3 sprigs.
Thyme. 2-3 sprigs fresh or ½ teaspoon dried.
Rosemary. 1 sprig.
Bay leaf. 2 pcs.
Vegetable oil. 50 g.
Salt. To taste.
Freshly ground black pepper. To taste.

Cooking Ossobuco

Let's start with the preparation of vegetables so you don't need to rush while dealing with meat after.
Dice the onion, celery and carrot. Chop the garlic finely enough as well.
Heat vegetable oil in a saucepan and put sliced vegetables. Add a little salt to make them brown faster and better.
Fry the vegetables for 5-6 minutes, until they start giving smell, soften a little and the onion starts to become transparent. Vegetables don't have to become very soft, that's why I fry them all together.
Turn off the heat and let's move on to the meat.
Wash and drain the meat. Tie each piece with a string so it retains the shape while cooking.
Heat up the vegetable oil in a wide frying pan.
Roll the tied pieces of meat in flour and spread on a well heated pan.
Fry the meat for 4-5 minutes on each side until brown.
Move the meat to the saucepan with the vegetables and stir all the contents. Add some salt.
Pour the wine to the frying pan where the meat was frying.
Let the wine boil at high heat.
Wait until the alcohol evaporates, it takes about 1-2 minutes.
Pour the wine into the saucepan with meat.
Tie parsley, rosemary, thyme and bay leaves together with a string.
If using fresh tomatoes, remove the skin. Make a cross-shaped cut on each tomato against the stalk and pour boiling water over the tomatoes for 3-4 minutes.
Then place the tomatoes in cold water to make the skin easy to remove.
Remove the skin and dice tomatoes into small pieces.
Add tomatoes and herbs to the saucepan.
Add broth, salt and pepper to taste and bring to a boil at high heat, then reduce the heat and cover tight.
Let the meat simmer at least 2-2½ hours or longer.
Spread the pieces of meat on a plate. It's not so easy because the meat has stewed to full softness. Use a wide spatula or a spoon.

Lamb with Quince and Dried Fruits

If you want to cook something fresh and fragrant, this dish will definitely suit you.

To prepare Lamb with Quince and Dried Fruits you will need

Lamb. Blade or leg will be best.
Quince.

Apple.
Onion.
Garlic.
Dried fruits.
Salt.
Black pepper freshly ground.

The proportions and number of products aren't specified deliberately. There was never and can't be ever any accuracy in this recipe which makes it even more brilliant!

Cooking Lamb with Quince and Dried Fruits

Preparation is very simple and there's no need for long description or explanations.
Slice apples and quinces and remove the seeds.
Chop the onion into large slices. Peel the garlic and leave the whole cloves.
Wash the dried fruits thoroughly.
Salt and pepper the meat to taste and put into a cooking bag together with all the other ingredients.
Close the bag tightly.
Then put the bag in the oven preheated to 180° C for 1½ h.
Serve with rice.

Pork with Beet Tops

Meat with this filling is tender as the filling does not let it dry out in the oven.

To make Pork with Beet Tops you will need

Beet leaves.
Chunks of pork neck, chops of 3-4 centimeters thick.

Grated cheese. Better to take the one with a distinctive flavor.
Salt.
Ground black pepper.
Your favorite spices for pork.

The amount of products isn't indicated deliberately. Choose according to your own appetite.

Cooking Pork with Beet Tops

In the chops, cut the largest pocket possible and rub it inside and out with salt, freshly ground black pepper and spices.
Then tenderize the meat on both sides.
Cut the beet leaves into thin strips.
Mix with grated cheese.
Fill the pork pockets with the filling tightly and completely. Clip the edges of the pockets with wooden toothpicks.
Wrap each piece in foil.
Then place the meat in the oven preheated to 200°C and after 30 minutes reduce the temperature to 180°C.
Cook about half an hour.
Serve hot.
The cold dish is very good cold for sandwiches as well.

Pork Ribs with Stewed Sauerkraut

A rich in flavor, purely very home-style dish. The cabbage should be specifically sour and its quality is crucial for this recipe.

To make Pork Ribs with Stewed Sauerkraut you will need

Pork ribs.
Sauerkraut.
Onion.
An apple.

Salt.
Freshly ground black pepper.

The amount of products isn't indicated deliberately. Choose according to your own appetite.

Cooking Pork Ribs with Sauerkraut

Chop a strip of pork ribs into pieces between the bones.
Chop the onion in half / quarter rings.
Heat up the oil in a saucepan and fry the pork ribs at high heat until crisp.
Then add the onion and fry it together with the meat until golden.
Slice the apple and add it to the saucepan. Lightly fry the apple with the meat.
Sprinkle with a little black pepper.
Chop sauerkraut into small pieces. You can lightly wash the cabbage from the brine if necessary. Add the cabbage to the saucepan.
If necessary, add a little brine from cabbage or just water for the cabbage to stew, not roast or boil. Cover and simmer at low heat for 1 ½ - 2 hours.
In the meantime check if the dish needs more seasoning.
Serve hot. We get very soft and tender pork, the meat falls off the bone easily. Having exchanged the tastes and smells, cabbage and pork acquire their own unique taste.
Sour cream greatly stresses the taste of the dish.

Pork Ribs with Honey

This dish allows getting a nice, hot, steamy dinner as well as a delicious sandwich or lunch, served cold. It engages very little time and effort and the only time-consuming part is roasting.

To make Pork Ribs with Honey you will need

1.2 kg of pork ribs.
Garlic. To taste.
Honey - 1 tablespoon.
Salt. To taste.
Soy sauce – 1 tablespoon.
Your preferred spices for meat.

Cooking Pork Ribs with Honey

Season the meat with salt, but not too much, keeping in mind the saltiness of soy sauce to be added later on.
Peel the garlic, cut each clove in half lengthwise, and stuff the pork with it. The most convenient way to do this is without removing the knife from the meat, just slipping down half garlic clove on the knife blade.
Mix a tablespoon of honey with a tablespoon of soy sauce.
Then cover a high baking pan with foil and spread a little honey and soy sauce mix.
Put the ribs on the foil skin down. Rub your favorite spices carefully over the meat with hands, and then spread the resulting honey and soy sauce mix over the entire piece of meat.
Cover everything with foil and put to a preheated 200°C oven. 20 minutes later reduce the temperature to 180°C and leave for another hour approximately. Cooking time actually depends on the size of the piece – my 1.2 kg piece was cooking for about half an hour. 20 minutes before the anticipated end, disclose the foil and turn over the piece skin-up. Put back in the oven and let the skin redden.
When the cooking time is up, open the oven door and leave the meat for 10-15 minutes in the oven.

Liver in Sour Cream

From time to time, the recipes from my childhood spring back to my mind.

To make Liver in Sour Cream you will need

A 700 g piece of liver. I prefer the beef one for this dish.
Onion.
Sour cream.
Butter for frying.
Water.
Salt.

As an option - flour or starch, preferably corn, to thicken the sauce.

The amount of products isn't indicated deliberately. Choose according to your own appetite.

Cooking the Liver in Sour Cream

First clean the liver from skins and channels and chop into small pieces.
Then slice the onion in quarter rings.
Melt the butter in a deep saucepan and add a little vegetable oil (for the butter not to burn). Put the onion, add a little salt.
Fry the onion until light golden.
Then add the liver and fry until light whitening.
Then, add boiling water to cover the liver and onion.
Cover the pan and simmer. Because the sauce is also important in this dish I simmer for about an hour. By this time the broth is becoming clear and the liver soft.
Then add a tablespoon of flour, stir it all vigorously with a spatula until the disappearance of lumps.
Then add 100-150 g of sour cream and salt.
Stir well and let the liver simmer for about a minute or two. The dish is done!
Let it cool for 15 minutes and serve.

Pilaf

Pilaf is a cult dish. Lots of lances were broken and swords were crossed over the recipe. I dare to say it's probably one of the few foods causing so many disputes all over the world. Here's the recipe I use but I'm far from claiming this recipe to be the Ultimate and True One.

To make Pilaf you will need

Lamb shoulder.
Onion.
Carrot.
Rice.
Garlic - carefully peeled from the external "paper" husk and root residues.
Spices for pilaf: Cumin, sumac, saffron, barberry to taste.
Vegetable oil.

The amount of products isn't indicated deliberately. Choose according to your own appetite.

Cooking the Pilaf

Chop the meat into pieces of the size of your choice. I prefer small, "one-bite" pieces. Slice onions into quarter rings, do not (!) grate carrots but cut them into thin strips with a knife.

Heat up a large pot and make the oil sizzle, almost haze. As soon as the oil starts sizzling, put the lamb bones and quickly fry them until golden brown.

Then add the rest of the meat partially, frying them quickly. It's crucial for the oil not to lose its temperature so the meat doesn't give away its juice. You should fry the meat, not stew it in its own juice. When the meat is browned, add chopped onion and carrots and fry.

Once the carrots become tender, add spices.

About 5-6 minutes later, pour boiling water over the contents of the pot to cover the meat almost completely and add the whole bulb of garlic.

Reduce the heat almost to a minimum and leave it for 40-50 minutes.

Season with salt profusely as we'll cook the rice in the stew which will absorb some salt.

Now, gently spread well washed rice over the meat with a slotted spoon. Spread over the entire surface evenly.

Then, pour boiling water also evenly on the rice. It's better to pour less water at the beginning and add more if necessary during cooking.

Reduce heat to medium and cook the rice. Don't stir it. From time to time heap the top layer of rice very carefully to the center with a slotted spoon and then gently flatten it. It's essential that the rice is cooked after the water has boiled away. If the rice is done but there's still some water, make holes from the top to the bottom with a slotted spoon to make water evaporate faster. If, however, water has boiled away and the rice is still wet – you can add 50 ml of boiling water and wait until absorbed.

When done, turn down the heat to very low and cover tight.

Simmer under the lid for 20-25 minutes. Then completely turn off the heat and uncover. Carefully loosen the rice, pull out the garlic.

Spread the contents of the pot on a large platter and serve.

Beef Stroganoff

Beef Stroganoff can be called an iconic meal and everyone prepares it in their own way. As the saying goes: "Many men, many minds."

To make Beef Stroganoff you will need

600 grams of beef.
400 grams of white mushrooms.
2-3 onion bulbs.
200 grams of sour cream.
Flour (very little) – about 1 tablespoon.
Salt and freshly ground black pepper to taste.
Odorless vegetable oil.

Cooking Beef Stroganoff

Chop the meat into small pieces.
Chop half of the onions you've taken.
Put the meat and the onion to a saucepan with preheated oil. Leave it covered to stew at low heat for around 50 minutes.
Dice the remaining onions.
Peel the mushrooms and slice them.
Fry the onion on the other frying pan until slightly golden, then add mushrooms. Cover the pan immediately on and cook at medium heat for 10 minutes.
After 10 minutes, open the lid and stir the mushrooms vigorously until evaporation of almost all moisture.
Check the meat. There should be some liquid in the saucepan. If it has boiled away, add a little boiling water.
Remember to add salt 10 minutes before the meal is ready.
When the mushrooms and onions are golden brown, add them to the meat.
After 2 minutes, check the sauce. If you think there is too little of it, add some water but not much.
Then, add the flour - about a tablespoon. Don't simply dump the whole spoon in one place, as it will be very tiresome to stir until smooth. Gently sprinkle the four over the surface of the meat and stir vigorously.
Wait 5 minutes then check again whether there's enough water.

Add the sour cream and stir again. Stew under cover at low heat for 5-7 minutes. The sour cream shouldn't stew for too long.

Oven-Grilled Rabbit

Rabbit has a very tender and soft meat that will make the dish aromatic and savory.

To make Grilled Rabbit you will need

500 ml of sour cream.
2 teaspoons of sea salt.
1 bundle of dill.
1 bundle of parsley.
1 rabbit carcass.

Cooking Grilled Rabbit

Take the rabbit carcass, wash it thoroughly and cut off the excess fat.
Season the carcass with salt and pepper. Chop the dill and parsley and rub them over the rabbit. Put the carcass to the bowl and pour sour cream.
The rabbit should be marinated for at least 2 hours but preferably all night.
Stick a skewer through the rabbit.
Preheat the oven to 200°C; put a roasting pan filled with water on the bottom of the oven (for the rabbit not to dry). Place the meat in a casserole and cook at 200° C for 30 minutes. Then turn on the grill function and cook for the another 40 minutes. Add some water if it has evaporated from the pan.
Serve with any vegetable salad as garnish.

14 culinary tricks that will take cooking to a restaurant level

Sometimes you might use the same recipe as the restaurant chef but somehow he gets a steak and you get a sole. Are you surprised? Well, you shouldn't be as you have to constantly learn and practice to finally become perfect in the kitchen.

Below you will find a few chefs' secrets on how to prepare delicious food quickly and easily.

While cooking a steak, do not flip the meat too often in the pan as you will lose a crisp coating and the meat will become dry because all the juice will flow into the pan instead of staying trapped in the meat. How will you know that it's time to flip the hamburger or steak? Shake the pan - if the meat "rides" on it, then it's ready.

Frying food for a long time using extra virgin olive oil is a big mistake: virgin oil begins to "burn" at a high temperature, making the dish less enriched and less tasty.
Bad eggs always float in the water so never eat them. Fresh eggs rest on the bottom of the bowl filled with water. If the egg is in the middle, then it's about two to three weeks old but it's still good to be eaten.
It's also a common mistake to chop freshly cooked meat - every meat dish needs to "take a rest" after cooking for a few minutes to be well done in the inside and to absorb the juice.
How to cook a delicious fish? Fry or grill it on lemon slices – no other scent or flavor gets inside and the dish is impregnated with the scent of citrus.
If you don't want the herbs to stick to the knife, sprinkle it a little with salt.

If you need a soft butter urgently (for sandwiches) and you just took it out of the fridge, here is a tip: put a glass of water in the microwave, let the glass get warm. Empty the glass and cover the butter with it, leaving it for a few minutes. Warm glass will make the butter soft.

Once opened wine may actually be kept for couple of days if closed with a stopper in an upright position, but don't exceed this time.

A common mistake is to put too many meat chops into one pan. If, instead of dry meat, you want a juicy one, try to leave a little space between the chops.

When making a casserole in the oven, sprinkle the dish with grated cheese only 5 minutes prior to taking it out of the oven. If you put the cheese at the very beginning, it will burn by the time the dish is ready and instead of beautifully gummy toppings you will get a crust that is impossible to chew.

For the chopping board not to slide put a kitchen towel under it.

Only warm milk can be poured to the mashed potatoes. Cold one gives a terribly gray color to the dish.

If you need many hard-boiled eggs (for a salad, for example), cooking them in the oven will be faster and easier than in a pot.

If you run out of mayonnaise and you desperately need it, just mix 1 egg and 150 ml of olive oil in a blender, seasoning with salt and pepper.

Bon Appetit!

Printed in Poland
by Amazon Fulfillment
Poland Sp. z o.o., Wrocław

25902569R00027